What Men NO
About Women
Are you sure you know what she's really thinking?

By David Selley

In *What Men NO About Women*, David Selley invites men to take a lighthearted but eye-opening look at the women in their lives. With wit, honesty, and just the right dose of humor, this interactive book guides readers through what truly matters—trust, empathy, communication, and more.

Through relatable insights, scorecards, and the occasional reality check, men are encouraged to listen better, love smarter, and laugh at the things they still don't quite understand. Whether you're dating, devoted, or just plain confused, this book is your guide to decoding modern relationships—with clarity, compassion, and comic relief.

First Edition: 2025

Other Books in the PAPA Series and Beyond: *See page 97.*

Publisher: Promptings Publishing - Fran Jessee has dedicated herself to bringing David Selley's PAPA Series to life. With meticulous attention to detail, Fran has edited and formatted David's Series to ensure that David's voice shines through on every page. Her commitment to preserving the authenticity of his narrative while enhancing readability makes this book a true reflection of David's experiences. For further information contact franjessee@gmail.com

Cover Design: David Selley
ISBN: 979-8-9995629-1-3
Printed in the United States of America

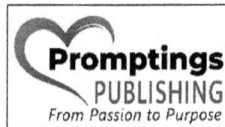

Promptings
PUBLISHING
From Passion to Purpose

May You Have

May your spring bring love in bloom,
With dreams to chase and hearts in tune.
May your summer shine with endless light,
Building memories both day and night.
May your autumn teach you to embrace,
The beauty of change, the gentlest grace.
May your winter wrap you in its glow,
A love that deepens as time does flow.
Through every season, may you find,
A bond that grows, heart and mind.
Together as one, steadfast and true,
Through all of life, may love guide you..

Aloha! From beautiful Hawaii!

David Selley

Dedication

To the men who've bravely attempted to
decode women, survived the eye-rolls,
and kept showing up anyway.

And to the women who put up with us...
thank you for your patience.

— David Selley

Foreword

Let's be honest...after 87 years on this planet, I've learned a few things.

One: Women are complicated.
Two: Men are often clueless.
Three: The combination of the two makes life gloriously confusing, hilarious, and beautiful.

Now, I'm not here to hand out relationship advice. Lord knows I've bungled enough to write *another* book just on that. But I *am* here to offer a simple tool...a fun, eye-opening little book that might just help you cut through the confusion and see what's really going on.

What Men NO About Women isn't about blaming, shaming, or trying to "fix" anyone. It's about laughing, learning, and seeing a bit more clearly. Think of it as your emotional cheat sheet...served with just enough humor to keep it from turning into a therapy session.

Inside, you'll find ten key traits (+1) that show up—or don't—in the women you know. You'll rate them, reflect on them, maybe shake your head (that's okay, it's part of the fun). And if I've done my job right, you'll come away knowing a whole lot more about the women in your life than you did before you opened this book.

Here's my hope: that somewhere in these pages, you find clarity. Maybe even healing. And definitely a few good laughs.

So grab your pen, grab a buddy, and let's find out what you really "NO" about women.

With respect, a grin, and all my best,

—David Selley

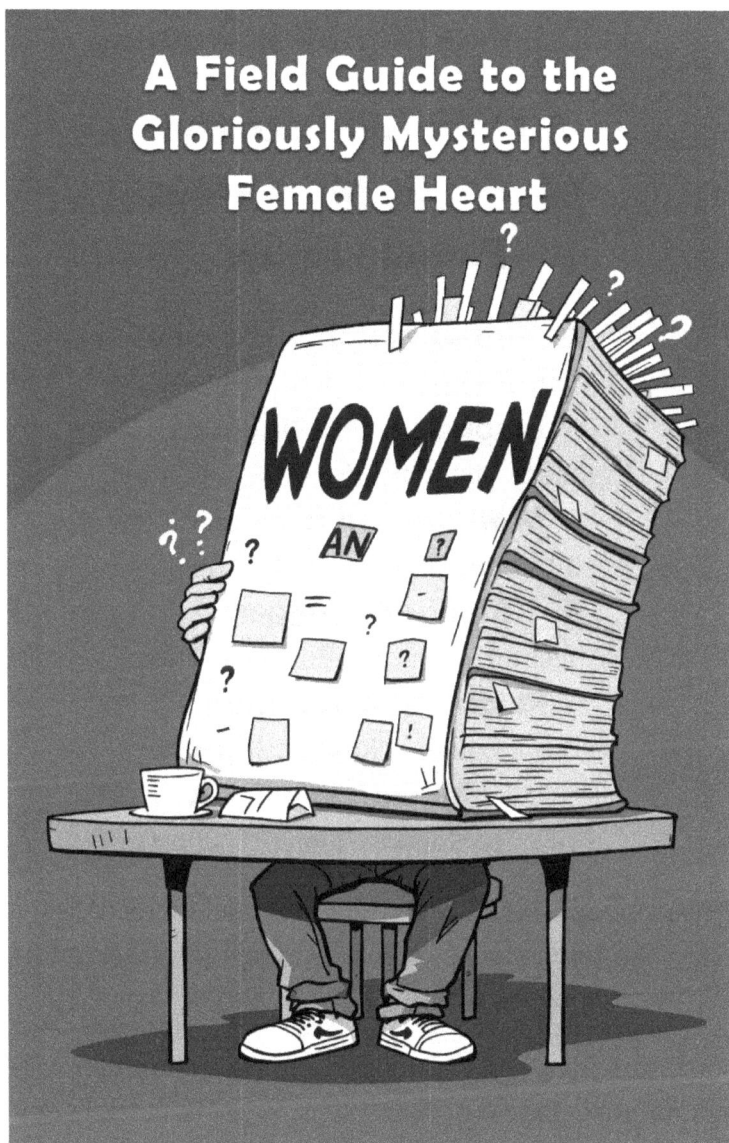
A Field Guide to the Gloriously Mysterious Female Heart

What Men NO About Women

A Field Guide to the Gloriously Mysterious Female Heart

20 Things You Should Know
(and She Wishes You Already Did)

Emotional Intelligence
Kindness. Listening. Honesty. Validation.

Womanhood Realities
Intuition. Independence. Growth.

Romantic Triggers
Affection. Attention. Romance. Tone.

Relationship Dynamics
Trust. Equality. Respect. Jealousy.

Modern Love
Presence. Support. Memory. Effort.

These 10 Essentials (+1) show up in all kinds of ways. To make them easier to spot (and avoid messing up), we've grouped them into 5 key categories.

Each one highlights traits and behaviors women care about most—like a decoder ring, but with more laughs and fewer regrets.

Introduction

10 Things Men Need to Know About Women...and
1 That Changes Everything.

We might not admit it, but we all have a mental list.

Somewhere between "Hey, want to grab a drink?" and her third "we need to talk" text, we start trying to figure out what *actually* matters.

Some guys have a real checklist (even if it's just in their heads). Others don't write anything down until it's too late...like during the post-breakup analysis over beers with friends who nod gravely and say, "Yeah, you really messed that one up."

We *think* we know what we want... or so we tell ourselves.

Usually, it starts with the obvious:
• She's attractive.

- She laughs at my jokes.
- She's into me enough to text back.

But real talk? What we notice first isn't always what *really* counts in the long run.

That's why this book is built around the 10 most essential things men need to understand about women—PLUS one bonus factor that rarely comes up on the first date... but quietly defines whether it'll ever work.

The +1?
Emotional Intelligence.
It's not glamorous until it's necessary.
She can be gorgeous, fun, and quote philosophy—but if no one can have a grown-up conversation without drama? Brother, think twice.
So here they are:
10 things to help you actually *get* women...
+1 that might just save your relationship
(or your sanity).

Let's dive in. Laugh, nod, wince in recognition, and maybe send an apology text to an ex (optional but recommended}.

Welcome to:
What Men NO About Women:
What Do You REALLY Know About the
Women in Your Life?

DISCLAIMER

This book contains humor, honesty, and potentially bruised egos. Side effects may include clarity, self-awareness, and spontaneous laughing fits. Recommended use: with a drink in hand and friends willing to call you out.

Why This Book Exists

A lot of men know the frustration of trying to understand women—and feeling like they're always getting it wrong.

One day you're told to open up, the next you're told to "be a man."

You're encouraged to talk about feelings, then asked why you're overreacting.

You want love, laughter, connection...but end up with confusion, cold shoulders, and arguments about the dishwasher.

This book won't magically solve every relationship mystery. But it *will* help you see what's really going on.

These 10+1 traits are the foundation of every good (or doomed) relationship. By reading, reflecting, and yes...even scoring yourself a bit...you'll give yourself permission to make better, stronger choices.

You're not broken. You're not clueless (well, maybe just a little). You just need better tools.

This book is one of them. Let's get to it.

A Note on the Title:
"What MEN NO About WOMEN"
Yes, it's NO, not "know."

Yes, it's NO, not "know."
In this book, NO isn't just a word —
it's survival, sanity, and sometimes... self-defense.

NO (noun, verb, exclamation, and exhausted sigh): The universal sound men make when faced with mixed signals, endless "we need to talk"s, shopping trips that last four hours, or "I'm fine" when she's very much *not* fine.

This title is a playful twist on what men *think* they know about women...and more importantly, what they've realized they can't fake understanding forever. Think of it as a salute to lessons learned the hard way, patience stretched to its limit, and humor absolutely required.

If you're a woman reading this...bless your kind heart. If you're a man ... welcome to the brotherhood. Let's get started.

"Whatever kind of woman you're trying to figure out—don't skip around. One chapter might feel spot-on today, another might hit differently tomorrow. Every page holds a clue, a laugh, or a truth bomb—because women (and relationships) are always evolving."

This book is part of
David Selley's
PAPA Book Series
A Guinness World Record Journey

—A 18-book collection of memoirs, relationsip wisdom, entrepreneurship and the International Entrepreneurs Assocation. As part of his Guinness World Record attempt to become the oldest author to publish the most books in one year. This series spans his journey across England, Canada and the USA. From overcoming hardships to building businesses and sustaining a 65-year marriage, these books capture the humor, resilience and wisdom of a life-well-lived. See the full list of book on page 97.

TABLE OF CONTENTS

Copyright ii

"May You Have" Poem iii

Foreword v

A Field Guide to the Gloriously
   Mysterious Female Heart vii

Introduction: 10 Things Men Need to Know About
   Women and 1 That Changes Everything ix

Why This Book Exists xii

A Note on the Title xiii

A Guinness World Record Journey xv

Part 1 – The 10 Essentials +1

Chapter 1 – Kindness 2

Chapter 2 – Listening 10

Chapter 3 – Security 15

Chapter 4 – Attention 22

Chapter 5 – Trust 28

Chapter 6 – Support 34

Chapter 7 – Affection 40

Chapter 8 – Independence 46

Chapter 9 – Intuition 52

Chapter 10 – Respect 58

Chapter 11 – Emotional Stability:
              +1 That Changes Everything 64

Part Two – Tools, Truths & Takeaways

Chapter 12 – Relationship Tools 71

   Tool #1: The 95/5 Method 72

   Tool #2: The Emotional Richter Scale 76

Chapter 13 – Score Summary + Reflection 81

TABLE OF CONTENTS *(Continued}*

Bonus Material

Bonus 1 – Say What You REALLY Wanted to Say 85
Bonus 2 – NO-O-Meter Wall of Fame (or Shame) 87
Bonus 3 – Sticky Note Truths 89
Bonus 4 – Review, Reflect & Share It 91

Final Word From David 92
A Guinness World Record Journey 95
Other Books in the PAPA Series 96
David's Favorite Books 99
My Creed – By Dean Alfange 101
About the Author 102

PART 1

WHAT MEN NO ABOUT WOMEN

The 10 Essentials
+1

Chapter 1

Kindness

"Kindness is love in action."

(And sometimes, it's just remembering you hate cilantro and didn't ask for a side of trauma with your tacos.)

David Says

"If she's kind when no one's watching?
You've struck gold.
If she's only kind when she wants something—or to win an argument later?
You've got a project, not a partner."

-Kindness is never accidental-

WHAT KINDNESS REALLY MEANS

- Kindness isn't about grand gestures or Instagram-worthy moments.
  It's the little things.
  The *everyday* things.
- It's how she speaks to you when she's mad.
  How she reacts when you forget something.
  How she treats you when you're not "useful."
- Kindness is her default setting—or it's not.
  It's holding space, not holding grudges.
  It's thinking of you *without* needing a reminder or a scoreboard.
- And if she's kind even when she doesn't have to be?
  That's not just a green flag—it's a whole forest.

What Kindness Looks Like
(*Real-Life Examples*)

▶ **Green Flag:**
She lets you finish your sentence without jumping in to correct it—then circles back later to show she actually understood.

▶ **Yellow Light:**
She listens... but you can feel her winding up to talk the entire time.

▶ **Red Flag:**
She says, *"Go ahead, I'm listening,"* but folds laundry,

texts her friend, and forgets everything you just said.

BEEN THERE, SAID THAT:

"If you open up and she weaponizes it later,
that's not a listener—
that's a lawyer prepping for trial."

Unofficial

No-O-Meter

How the Women in My Life Score
(A completely biased, emotionally-charged, snack-fueled ranking system)

We all know some women deserve statues... and some deserve a Post-it note that says "NOPE" in giant red letters.

So here's a handy scoring system—based on real-life interactions, emotional survival, and pizza-delivery gratitude—to help you see how the women in your life stack up.

How to Score Your Gals —

Name/Nickname	Score (1–10)	Quick Example or Story
Mom	9	Always heard me—even when I didn't say much.
Girlfriend	4	Listens when I talk... then brings it up at the worst times.
Wife	7	Good listener, but sometimes talks over the solution.
Sister	10	Doesn't just hear—she gets it.
Friend	6	Says "I'm listening," but can't repeat back what I said.

The Official
NO-O-Meter Rating Scale

Before you fill out your chart, answer these extremely scientific questions for each woman in your life. Add up the points and discover the truth.

Ask yourself:

✓ Speaks to you with respect—
even when she's mad? → **+2**

✓ Checks on you when you're quiet—not just when you're useful? → **+2**

✓ Does little things for you without needing a spotlight? → **+2**

✗ Uses sarcasm as her love language (but it's really just sharp)? → **–2**

✗ Keeps score of everything she's ever done for you? → **–1**

✓ Shows up when you need her—even if it's inconvenient? → **+2**

✓ Makes you feel safe being yourself? → **+1**

✗ Dismisses your stress because "hers is worse"? → **–1**

✓ Offers real kindness, not performative niceness? → +1

Score out of 10.
No decimals. No editing.
Petty observations are welcome.
Score out of 10.
No decimals. No do-overs. Petty is allowed.

Your Turn!
Fill in Your Personal NO-O-Meter

Name/Nickname	Score (1–10)	Quick Example or Story

Name/Nickname	Score (1–10)	Quick Example or Story

(P.S. Showing them your answers is optional. Framing it on the fridge? That's on you.)

RED FLAG ⚑ RADAR:

Kindness Edition

Watch out for these signs of **fake listening:**

Watch out for these signs that her "kindness" might just be camouflage:

⚑ She's nice only when others are watching.

⚑ Says "I'm just being honest" when she's actually being mean.

⚑ Keeps score of everything she's ever done for you— and reminds you.

⚑ Uses guilt as a go-to tool instead of grace.

⚑ Calls you "sensitive" when you express hurt.

⚑ Does nice things... but makes sure you know how inconvenient it was.

GREEN FLAG ▶ SIGNALS:

Here's what real, no-strings-attached
kindness actually looks like:

✓ She remembers the little things—without you
having to ask.

✓ Shows patience when you're not at your best.

✓ Checks in on you just because—not for praise.

✓ Is kind even when she's tired, stressed, or annoyed.

✓ Speaks to you with respect—even in disagreement.

✓ Gives without keeping score—and receives without
entitlement.

IF SHE SCORES A 9 OR 10...
You lucky devil.
Celebrate her.
Buy her flowers.
Or at least say thank you with more than
just a thumbs-up emoji.

IF SHE SCORES A 3 OR BELOW...
Consider using the **95/5 Method**
(see Chapter 11).
Or possibly a solo vacation. For her.
Without cell service.

YOUR NOTES, RANTS, OR PRAISE

Praise her, roast her, write your next therapy session—no one's judging.

Chapter 2

Listening

"Listening is love with both ears open."

❤❤

(Especially when she doesn't cut you off to tell a better version of your own story.)

WHAT LISTENING REALLY MEANS

*Honesty in a relationship isn't just about whether he lies—it's about **how** he tells the truth.*

Listening isn't about silence. It's about presence.

Does she actually hear you—or just wait for her turn to talk? Does she lean in with curiosity—or glaze over until the topic changes?

Real listening means:
No interruptions.
No fixing
No "you're overreacting."

It means hearing not just your words—but what's underneath them.

Because when a man feels heard, he lets his guard down. And when he doesn't?

He shuts down. Or worse—stops trying to connect at all.

David Says

😉

"A woman who listens without judgment? Rare. One who says, 'Are you done?' mid-sentence? Run. Or at least stop talking."

WHAT LISTENING LOOKS LIKE (REAL-LIFE EXAMPLES)

➤ Green Flag:
She sets her phone down, looks at you, and says, "That sounds hard—tell me more."
➤ Yellow Light:
She nods while you talk... but you can see her mentally drafting her reply.

🚩 Red Flag:
You say, "This is important to me," and she replies, "Can
we not do this right now?"

BEEN THERE, SAID THAT:

"If you feel like you're talking to the wall—
don't be surprised when the wall never hugs you back."

Your

No-O-Meter
Listening EDITION

Scoring time!

Rate the women in your life **1–10** based on how well
they actually listen—without interrupting, tuning out,
or using your words against you later.

Name/Nickname	Score (1–10)	Quick Example or Story
Mom	9	Always made space for my thoughts—even dumb ones.

Name/Nickname	Score (1–10)	Quick Example or Story
Girlfriend	4	Listens just long enough to form a comeback.
Wife	7	Mostly listens... unless there's a commercial she likes.
Sister	8	Honest, focused, and actually remembers what I say.
Friend	6	Hears me, but sometimes gives TED Talks I didn't ask for.

THE NO-O-METER SCALE:
Listening EDITION

Ask yourself...

✓ She lets you finish your thought without interrupting → **+2**

✓ Makes eye contact and stays present → **+2**

✓ Remembers things you said last week → **+1**

✓ Asks thoughtful follow-up questions → **+2**

✓ Doesn't try to "fix" your feelings → **+1**

✗ Cuts you off to tell a better version of *her* story → **–2**

✗ Says "I'm listening" while texting → **–1**

✘ Brings up what you shared...
later, in an argument → **-2**
✘ Says "You never talk to me," but talks over you → **-1**

Add it up.
Then ask:
Does she really *hear* you—or just wait for her turn to talk?

Circle the score. Then sit with it.

IF SHE SCORES A 9 OR 10...
Pop the champagne—or at least look her in the eye and say, *"Thanks for really hearing me."*
You've got a rare one. Don't take it for granted.

IF SHE SCORES A 3 OR BELOW...
You're not crazy—just constantly misunderstood.
Ask yourself:
Are you talking... or just background noise in her show?

***(Feeling unheard is frustrating. Feeling erased?
That's a whole different kind of lonely.)***

YOUR NOTES, RANTS, OR PRAISE

(If she's not really listening, why are you still explaining?)

_____

_____

_____

_____

_____

_____

_____

_____

_____

_____

_____

_____

Chapter 3

Security

> ## "**Security** isn't just safety...
> ## it's peace."

💕

(And no, it's not just about locking the front door.)

WHAT **Security** REALLY MEANS

Security to a woman isn't just about physical protection. It's about how she *feels*—with you, and because of you. Does she relax when she's with you?

Does she feel like you've got her back, even when life is messy?

Security shows up in the small things:
- Following through on what you say.

- Letting her vent without fixing.
- Being the calm in the chaos—not the cause of it.

It's not about money. It's not about muscles. It's about emotional consistency.

When she feels safe, she blossoms.

When she doesn't, she guards her heart—and you'll feel the distance.

David Says

Look, most women don't want a superhero. They want a man who makes them feel safe to be themselves.

If she's jumpy, quiet, or always apologizing for her feelings?

It's not about her being "too sensitive"… It's about her her not feeling secure.

WHAT Security LOOKS LIKE
(REAL-LIFE EXAMPLES)

(REAL-LIFE EXAMPLES)
▶ Green Flag:
She's not afraid to be vulnerable—
even when she's emotional or upset.

▶ **Yellow Light:**
She trusts you with most things...
but still keeps a backup plan.
▶ **Red Flag:**
She triple-checks your story—and her GPS—before
opening up.

NO ONE ASKED, BUT HERE'S MY OPINION
If she's constantly "fine,"
but never really *free*—
you might not be the safe place she needs.

RATE YOUR WOMAN - **Security**

Name/Nickname	Score (1–10)	Quick Example or Story
Wife	9	Tells me everything—even the stuff that's hard to say.
Girlfriend	6	Opens up sometimes, but always with a shield.
Ex	2	Said "nothing's wrong" while packing a suitcase.
Friend	10	Says I make her feel calm in the middle of chaos.

No-O-Meter
Security EDITION

Ask Yourself...

✓ She tells you the truth—
even when she's upset → **+2**

✓ She relaxes around you → **+2**

✓ She doesn't second-guess your intentions → **+1**

✓ She trusts you with her emotions → **+2**

✓ She feels safe being fully herself → **+1**

✗ She walks on eggshells around your moods → **–2**

✗ Says "I'm fine" but shuts down emotionally → **–1**

✗ Doesn't share until things are falling apart → **–2**

✗ Doubts your words because your actions don't
match → **–1**

Add it up. Circle the score.
Then ask yourself:
*Is she at ease with you—or just trying
not to upset you?*

IF SHE SCORES A 9 OR 10...
You're doing something right.
When a woman feels safe, her love deepens.
Protect that connection—it's rare.

IF SHE SCORES A 3 OR BELOW...
It's not about what she says.
It's about what she **can't** say—
because she doesn't feel safe enough.

(She might still care.
She just doesn't trust you with the parts
that matter most.)

YOUR NOTES, RANTS, OR PRAISE

(If she doesn't feel safe with you, nothing else matters.)

Chapter 4

Attention

**"If you give her your full Attention,
you might just earn her full
affection."**

(Unless his idea of humor is fart jokes at dinner...
then we need to talk.)

WHAT Attention REALLY MEANS

Attention isn't just saying "uh-huh" while scrolling
through emails.
It's about *presence.*
It's how she knows if you're tuned in... or tuned out.
It's the difference between being her partner — or just
her plus-one in life.

A woman who feels seen and heard:
- Softens
- Connects
- Gives you the best version of herself

Ignore her? She'll start wondering why she's even there.

David Says
😉

Let me tell you — women don't need a man who's perfect. They need a man who's *present.*

If you can't put your phone down, your ego aside, or your agenda on pause to *really* hear her — don't be surprised when she checks out emotionally.

And brother, when a woman checks out emotionally... you'll feel it in the air, the bed, and the fridge.

WHAT **Attention** LOOKS LIKE
(REAL-LIFE EXAMPLES)

▶ Green Flag:
You notice when she's quiet — and ask why *before* she has to tell you.
(And you don't try to fix it. You just *be there.*)

▶ Yellow Light:
You listen — sort of — but forget half of it by morning.
("Wait... when did you say your mom was coming to stay?")

⚑ Red Flag:
You interrupt, correct, or dismiss her —
especially in front of others.
(It's not just rude. It's relationship sabotage.)

FROM THE GUY WHO'S SEEN IT ALL

"If she has to compete with your phone, your schedule, or your pride...she'll eventually stop competing."

RATE YOUR WOMAN – Attention

Name/Nickname	Score (1–10)	Quick Example or Story
Me (honestly)	6	I hear her, but I'm working on actually *listening.*
My buddy Mike	3	Nods a lot. Hears nothing. Still single.
My dad	8	Mom never had to repeat herself. That's saying something.
My ex	2	Claimed I "talk too much." Now he talks to himself.

No-O-Meter
Attention EDITION

Ask Yourself

✓ She tells you what's on her mind—without needing a breakdown first → **+2**

✓ She knows you're actually listening—not just hearing → **+2**

✓ She feels like her feelings *land* with you, not bounce off → **+1**

✓ She opens up because she feels emotionally seen → **+2**

✓ She doesn't need to fight for your focus → **+1**

✗ She checks out because you always check your phone → **–2**

✗ She stops talking halfway through because you've already tuned out → **–1**

✗ She only shares when things are falling apart → **–2**

✗ She tests you to see if you're actually paying attention → **–1**

Add it up. Circle the score.
Then ask yourself:
Is she sharing with you—or just used to not being heard?

IF SHE SCORES A 9 OR 10...
You're doing something rare.
When a woman feels *seen* and emotionally
received, she glows.
Stay curious. Stay present. It matters.

IF SHE SCORES A 3 OR BELOW...
It's not about her volume.
It's about whether you *noticed* before she went quiet.
(She might still be talking...
but she stopped expecting you to really hear it.)

YOUR NOTES, RANTS, OR PRAISE

*"If she has to keep repeating herself, she'll eventually
stop talking — and that's when you
should start worrying."*

Chapter 5

Trust

"

"Trust isn't built in grand gestures— it's built in small moments when she sees you *mean it*."

(And if she flinches when you say "trust me"... there's history there.)

WHAT Trust REALLY MEANS

Trust isn't just "I've never cheated." It's deeper.

It's about consistency, character, and follow-through. Does she feel safe with you—not just physically, but emotionally?

28

A woman trusts you when:
- You say what you mean and mean what you say
- You follow through on promises (even the boring ones)
- You don't make her feel foolish for being honest

Trust is built over time, but it can break in a moment. And once it's cracked?

You'd better have more than duct tape and good intentions.

And bad attitude? Well... that stuff spreads faster than a cold at Christmas.

David Says

Let me be straight with you—
Women want to feel like they can lean in without falling flat.
If she hesitates before opening up...
If she triple-checks your words against your actions...
She's not "dramatic." She's watching.
Because somewhere along the line, someone taught her that "I got you" doesn't always mean what it should.
If you want her trust, earn it.
If you have it already—guard it like gold.

WHAT **Trust** LOOKS LIKE
(REAL-LIFE EXAMPLES)
▶ Green Flag:
She opens up about something painful — and trusts
you enough not to fix it, just hear her.
▶ Yellow Light:
She says "it's fine," but you can tell it's not — and she's
not sure she can bring it up.
▶ Red Flag:
She hides things, deletes messages, or avoids emotional
conversations entirely.
(That's not mystery — that's a warning.)

STRAIGHT FROM THE MAN MANUAL
(PAGE MISSING)
(That no one gave you, but we're writing it anyway)

"A woman who trusts you will show up fully.
But if she starts editing herself around you,
you're not just losing her words — you're losing *her*."

RATE YOUR WOMAN – **Trust**

Name/Nickname	Score (1–10)	Quick Example or Story
Wife	9	Tells me what she needs — and trusts I'll try.
Girlfriend	6	Opens up slowly. I'm learning to earn it.

Name/Nickname	Score (1–10)	Quick Example or Story
Ex	3	Said everything was fine until she ghosted me emotionally.
Sister	8	Always honest — even when it stings. That's trust.

No-O-Meter
Trust EDITION

Ask yourself:

✔ She tells you the truth — even when it's hard → +2

✔ She lets her guard down around you → +2

✔ She believes what you say the first time → +1

✔ She shares her real thoughts without fear → +2

✘ She checks your tone before answering → –1

✘ She holds back or filters everything → –2

✘ She says "I'm fine" when clearly she's not → –1

✘ She assumes you'll disappoint her → –2

Add it up. And then ask:

Have you made it safe for her to trust you —
or just safe for her to smile and stay quiet?

IF SHE SCORES A 9 OR 10...
That's a woman who's emotionally all in.
Respect that. Don't make her regret it.

IF SHE SCORES A 3 OR BELOW...
If her trust is missing, it's not always about *you*.
But if she's still here —
you've got a chance to fix it. Start now.

YOUR NOTES, RANTS, OR PRAISE

If she's always smiling but never sharing,
you don't have trust — you have a performance.
And it's one standing ovation away from being over.

v

Chapter 6

Support

"Support doesn't always sound like 'I got you.' Sometimes it looks like showing up—again."

(And if she only cheers for you in public but checks out in private... pay attention.)

WHAT Support REALLY MEANS

A good personality doesn't mean she's the loudest laugh in the room (though bonus points if she brings dessert).

Support isn't about grand declarations or perfectly filtered Instagram posts.

It's the steady stuff.

Does she *stand beside you* — or just *stand by* when it's convenient?

Real support from a woman means:
- She believes in your potential — even before the results show up
- She encourages you without controlling you
- She's in your corner, not just on your case
- Support isn't silent. It's not pushy.

It's that steady "I'm with you" that makes you want to be better — not because you have to, but because you're *safe to try.*

> The opposite? Sarcasm as a defense, mood swings as a personality trait, or just being... me.

David Says

Listen — men carry pressure like backpacks full of bricks.

You don't always need someone to take the load off... But it sure helps to have someone who walks beside you and says, "You're not crazy. You're not lazy. And no, you're not alone.

If a woman backs your dreams, respects your struggles,

and doesn't make your ambition feel like a threat...
Hold on to her.

But if she only supports the version of you that *pleases her*? That's not a partner. That's a project manager.

WHAT **Support** LOOKS LIKE
(REAL-LIFE EXAMPLES)

▶ Green Flag:
She reminds you of who you are on your worst days —
not just your best ones.
(And somehow makes you believe it again.)
▶ Yellow Light:
She encourages you... until it gets inconvenient for her.
("Wait — this new job means *less* time with me?")
▶ Red Flag:
She mocks your goals, minimizes your wins, or plays
the "you'll probably fail" card.
(That's not tough love. That's insecurity with lipstick.)

NO ONE ASKED, BUT HERE'S MY OPINION

If she can only cheer you on when she's in the spotlight,
you don't have a partner — you have competition.

And competition doesn't build empires together.
It tears them apart.

RATE YOUR WOMAN - **Support**

Name/Nickname	Score (1–10)	Quick Example or Story
Wife	9	Encouraged me to start my business — and brought me snacks while I figured it out.
Girlfriend	6	Wants to be supportive, but struggles when she's not in control.
Ex	3	Told me I dream too big. And then complained when I didn't try.
Sister	10	Always believes in me. Even when I don't. Especially then.

No-O-Meter
Support EDITION

✓ Encourages without controlling → **+2**

✓ Believes in your ideas (even weird ones) → **+2**

✓ Listens without always trying to fix → **+2**

✓ Celebrates your wins — big and small → **+1**

✓ Respects your pace, your process → **+1**

✗ Criticizes your ambition or goals → **−2**

✗ Withdraws when you struggle → **−1**

✗ Makes support conditional → **−2**

✗ Feels competitive instead of collaborative → **−1**

Add it up. Then ask:
Does her support lift you — or limit you?

IF SHE SCORES A 9 OR 10...
That's a partner who builds your belief bank.
Keep showing up for her the way she shows up for you.

IF SHE SCORES A 3 OR BELOW...
If every risk you take becomes an argument...
you're not in a partnership.
You're in performance mode. And that's exhausting.

38

YOUR NOTES, RANTS, OR PRAISE

*If her "support" feels like pressure in disguise,
you'll spend your life performing —
not growing.*

Chapter 7

Affection

"If she pulls away every
time you reach for her,
there's more going on
than you think."

(And no, affection doesn't just mean sex. Nice try.)

WHAT **Affection** REALLY MEANS

Affection isn't just hugs and kisses. It's how she expresses closeness — and how she wants to feel yours.

Does she reach for your hand in public?
Send sweet texts out of nowhere?

Lean into you when you talk, not just when you touch?
Real affection is:

- Warmth without expectation
- Gentle connection, not just physicality
- A sign she feels safe, seen, and valued

If affection feels forced, absent, or only appears when things are going her way — don't ignore it. That's not just a mood.

That's not just a mood. That's a message.

David Says

Look — not all women are touchy-feely. But all women need to *feel* something to offer affection freely. If she's gone cold, it's rarely random. Something's off. It could be unspoken hurt, emotional distance, or simply not feeling appreciated.

And trust me — if she stops reaching for you, it's not because she doesn't need connection. It's because she stopped expecting it from *you.*

WHAT **Affection** LOOKS LIKE
(REAL-LIFE EXAMPLES)

▶ Green Flag:
She hugs you after a fight. Not because everything's perfect, but because connection still matters.

▶ **Yellow Light:**
She used to initiate affection —
now it only happens if *you* start it.
(And even then, she stiffens like a board.)
▶ **Red Flag:**
She avoids your touch, avoids your eyes,
and avoids telling you why.
(Affection isn't dead...
but the relationship might be on life support.)

JUST SAYIN'...
If affection feels like a reward instead of a rhythm,
something deeper is missing.
Check in — not just with her body, but with her heart.

RATE YOUR WOMAN – Affection

Name/Nickname	Score (1–10)	Quick Example or Story
Wife	8	Always kisses my shoulder when she walks past. It's small, but it means a lot.
Girlfriend	5	Used to cuddle on the couch. Now she sits at the other end. Still figuring it out.
Ex	2	Said she "wasn't the affectionate type." Turns out she just wasn't into *me*.

Name/Nickname	Score (1–10)	Quick Example or Story
Friend Who Flirts	9	Hugs like she means it. Makes me wonder what if.

No-O-Meter
Affection EDIT

✔ Initiates physical closeness → +2

✔ Responds warmly to your touch → +2

✔ Sends sweet words or small gestures → +2

✔ Shows consistent emotional connection → +1

✔ Feels safe and relaxed around you → +1

✗ Pulls away from affection → –2

✗ Says "I'm just not affectionate" but used to be → –2

✗ Uses affection only when she wants something → –1

✗ Shuts down physical touch altogether → –1

Add it up. Then ask:
Is she connected — or just co-existing?
Score it. Sniff test optional. Soap required.

IF SHE SCORES A 9 OR 10...

You've got a partner who *wants* to connect —
emotionally and physically.
Appreciate that. Return it daily.

IF SHE SCORES A 3 OR BELOW...

If her affection has vanished without explanation,
don't just brush it off.
Ask why. Listen hard.
And be ready to hear more than you expected.

YOUR NOTES, RANTS, OR PRAISE

*If the only time she touches you is to pass the remote...
that's not affection — that's a sign.*

Chapter 8

Independence

**"An independent woman doesn't need you...
she *chooses* you."**

(And if that scares you...
you've got some inner lifting to do.)

WHAT Independence REALLY MEANS

Independence isn't about being bossy, cold, or "too much." It's about knowing who she is — and not needing a relationship to complete her.

A truly independent woman:
- Makes her own decisions
- Handles her own money
- Enjoys your company, not your control

She's not waiting for permission, applause, or rescue.
She's building a life — and hoping you're strong enough to walk beside her, not ahead or behind.

David Says
☺

Independent doesn't mean she doesn't *care.* It means she's not afraid to be alone — which is why she's more careful about who she lets in.

If you find a woman who handles her business, honors her boundaries, and isn't afraid to call out your nonsense... Don't call her difficult. Call her a blessing... Because she'll lift you, not lean on you.

WHAT **Independence** LOOKS LIKE
(REAL-LIFE EXAMPLES)

▶ **Green Flag:**
She makes plans, keeps goals, and *includes* you—
without needing to be rescued.

▶ **Yellow Light:**
She says she's independent...
but constantly seeks approval.
(There's strength there, but also healing
still in progress.)

▶ **Red Flag:**
Uses "I don't need anyone" as a weapon, not a truth.
(Cue emotional shutdown anytime you get too close.)

FROM THE GUY WHO'S SEEN IT ALL

"An independent woman doesn't play games. She's got her own rules — and her own joy. If you're just looking to be needed, you'll miss the beauty of being *chosen*."

RATE YOUR WOMAN –
Independence

Name/Nickname	Score (1–10)	Quick Example or Story
Wife	9	Runs her own business, remembers birthdays, and still has time to help me fix my résumé.
Girlfriend	6	Smart and capable, but second-guesses herself more than she should. I cheer her on.
Ex	3	Said she was independent but needed constant validation. Draining.
Sister	10	Built a life, a career, and a cabin in the woods. Still texts me to check in. Legend.

No-O-Meter
Independence EDITION

✓ Makes her own choices confidently → **+2**
✓ Has passions, goals, or a career
she cares about → **+2**
✓ Doesn't rely on you for happiness → **+2**
✓ Sets boundaries kindly but firmly → **+1**
✓ Takes care of herself emotionally
and financially → **+1**
✗ Sees interdependence as weakness → **–2**
✗ Uses "I'm fine" to avoid vulnerability → **–2**
✗ Resents compromise or teamwork → **–1**
✗ Plays power games to "prove" independence → **–1**

Score it. Then ask:
Are you supporting her strength — or insecure around it?

IF SHE SCORES A 9 OR 10...
That's a partner who knows her worth.
Love her boldly — not because she needs it,
but because she deserves it.

IF SHE SCORES A 3 OR BELOW...
She may say she's independent,
but the relationship feels more like a rescue mission
than a partnership.
Check if you're helping her grow —
or enabling her stuckness.

YOUR NOTES, RANTS, OR PRAISE

*If her idea of independence means
shutting you out completely...
she's not strong — she's just hiding.
And connection doesn't live in hiding.*

Chapter 9

Intuition

"A woman's **Intuition** isn't a
guessing game —
it's a warning system with Wi-Fi."

💕

(And if you keep dismissing it, you'll be shocked
when she's right. Again.)

WHAT **Intuition** REALLY MEANS

Intuition isn't about magic or mood swings.
It's her inner compass — and spoiler: it usually works
better than yours.

A woman's intuition shows up when:

- Something feels off, even if it looks fine
- Someone says all the right words... but her gut says *nope*
- You say "nothing's wrong," and she knows *everything* is

She doesn't need evidence.
She doesn't need proof.
She just *knows.*

Ignore it, and you're not just disrespecting her —
you're ignoring one of the sharpest tools she brings to the table.

David Says

Listen — I've learned this the hard way:
When a woman says, "Something doesn't feel right,"
she's not being dramatic. She's being *accurate.*

Intuition is like her emotional radar. It scans your tone, your energy, your pauses... and yes, even your texts.

If you want to build trust, stop dismissing her instincts. Start asking what they're telling her — and maybe... start listening.

WHAT **Intuition** LOOKS LIKE
(REAL-LIFE EXAMPLES)

▶ **Green Flag:**

She speaks up when something feels off — calmly, clearly, and early.

▶ **Yellow Light:**

She senses something's wrong but doesn't say anything until it explodes.

(That's not drama. That's suppressed wisdom.)

▶ **Red Flag:**

She's so used to being ignored or gaslit that she no longer trusts her own gut.

(Make no mistake: that's not peace. That's resignation.)

NO ONE ASKED, BUT HERE'S MY OPINION

If you treat her intuition like it's a problem, she'll eventually treat *you* like the problem. And buddy, that's a vibe shift you won't enjoy.

RATE YOUR WOMAN – **Intuition**

Name/Nickname	Score (1–10)	Quick Example or Story
Wife	9	Knew I wasn't okay before I said a word. And she was right.

Name/Nickname	Score (1–10)	Quick Example or Story
Girlfriend	6	Sometimes senses things but doubts herself. I'm helping her trust it again.
Ex	3	Called me "paranoid." Turned out I wasn't the one lying.
Sister	10	Can spot a fake smile across a parking lot. Should be in the CIA.

No-O-Meter
Intuition EDITION

✓ Trusts her gut and shares honestly → **+2**

✓ Picks up on energy shifts, not just words → **+2**

✓ Calls things out early — not after a blow-up → **+2**

✓ Balances instinct with logic → **+1**

✓ Uses intuition to *connect*, not control → **+1**

✗ Doubts herself because no one listens → **−2**

✘ Lets red flags slide to keep the peace → **-2**
✘ Is accused of being "too sensitive" too often → **-1**
✘ Feels like she has to prove what she *feels* → **-1**

Add it up. Then ask yourself:
Are you safe for her truth — or just comfortable with silence?

IF SHE SCORES A 9 OR 10...
She's emotionally dialed in.
That's not a challenge — that's a gift.
Honor it.

IF SHE SCORES A 3 OR BELOW...
If her intuition's buried under self-doubt,
it may be because no one ever believed her.
Want to be different? Start now.

YOUR NOTES, RANTS, OR PRAISE

If you keep brushing off her instincts,
she'll stop sharing them —
and one day, she'll just leave without explaining why.
Because deep down...
she knew.

Chapter 10

Respect

"**Respect** isn't optional. It's oxygen in disguise."

(And sometimes, it's just not correcting her for the third time about the gas mileage on your truck.)

WHAT **Respect** REALLY MEANS

Respect isn't just earned. It's expressed. Daily. Respect isn't just about opening doors or complimenting her intelligence during trivia night.

It's about how you speak to her. How you disagree with her. How you make her feel even when you think she's wrong.

It's not interrupting, not talking down, and not rolling your eyes when she's passionate about something you don't get.

Respect means taking her seriously—even when she's emotional. It's believing she has her own wisdom, her own truth, and her own strength.

And if she respects you too? You'll feel like a king—with zero crowns involved.

David Says
☺

"You can't love someone you secretly don't respect. And you can't stay with someone who makes you feel small." You need a mirror.

WHAT Respect LOOKS LIKE
(Real-Life Examples)
▶ **Green Flag:**
You disagree—and she still listens like
what you say matters.
▶ **Yellow Light:**
She laughs off your opinions around others "as a joke."
▶ **Red Flag:**
She finishes your sentences, contradicts your choices,
and corrects your story in front of your friends.
Every. Time.

BEEN THERE, SAID THAT:
"If she treats you like a project instead of a partner—it's not love, it's a lecture."

Unofficial
How the Women in My Life Score:
Respect

Respect doesn't always wear a name tag. Sometimes it's hidden in tone, timing, and how much space she gives you to be *you*.

Time to rate how respected you really feel.

Name/Nickname	Score (1–10)	Quick Example or Story
Mom	8	*Always trusted me to make my own choices.*
Girlfriend	5	*Loves me, but talks over me when I'm not agreeing.*
Ex	3	*Constant corrections. Always made me feel stupid.*
Boss/Friend	9	*Doesn't always agree—but always hears me out.*
Sister	7	*Teases me, but has my back when it counts.*

No-O-Meter
Respect EDITION

Score each woman in your life based on how much respect you *feel*—not just what they say.

Ask yourself:

✔ Listens without mocking your ideas? → **+2**

✔ Honors your boundaries without guilt trips? → **+2**

✔ Lets you lead sometimes without power games? → **+1**

✗ Cuts you off or talks over you constantly? → **–2**

✔ Trusts your judgment in tough moments? → **+1**

✗ Publicly criticizes you or makes
you the punchline? → **–2**

✔ Includes you in big decisions? → **+2**

✔ Asks for your opinion because she *wants* it, not just to check a box? → **+2**

Total Score: _____ / 10

IF SHE SCORES A 9 OR 10...
You've created a safe space where
she can fully be herself.
No performance. No pretending. Just real.

That's rare.
Keep showing up that way.

IF SHE SCORES A 3 OR BELOW...
If she doesn't feel seen, she won't stay.
Respect isn't about rescuing her.
You don't need to fix her.
You just need to believe her.

YOUR NOTES, RANTS, OR PRAISE

"This is where you say what you couldn't—because being dismissed hurts more than being wrong."

Chapter 11

Emotional Stability

"The real test is how she acts when she's disappointed — not when she's adored."

(And if every mood shift feels like a storm warning... it's time to check the emotional forecast.)

WHY THIS IS THE +1 THAT CHANGES EVERYTHING

You can handle quirks. You can handle sass. You can even handle a strong opinion or three. But if she melts down, shuts down, or spins out every time things don't go her way?

You're not in a relationship — you're in a survival simulation.

Emotional stability isn't about being emotionless. It's about handling emotion *with maturity* — and not making everyone else suffer for it.

This is the trait that makes all the others stick. Without it? Even kindness, passion, or beauty become landmines.

WHY THIS TRAIT MATTERS MOST
This is the one.
The trait that makes or breaks it all.

You can laugh together, build together, even love deeply — but if her go-to reaction to stress is withdrawal, attack, or a code-red meltdown ... you'll never feel fully safe.

Stability doesn't mean she's calm all the time. It means she knows how to *own* her emotions — not unleash them like emotional glitter bombs.

David Says

You want passion? Great.

An emotionally grounded woman is a force of nature... in the best way. She can feel deeply and still stay present. She can disagree without destroying.. She can be sad, mad, or scared ... and still be safe to be around.

If she explodes, retreats, or blames you every tme life gets hard . . . that's not emotion . . . that is volatility. And volatillity doesn't build a future . . . it just burns bridges.

WHAT **Emotional Stability** LOOKS LIKE

► **Green Flag:**
She talks things through, listens when you speak, and doesn't weaponize silence or tears.
► **Yellow Light:**
She *says* she's fine...
but the tension is louder than words.
(You're decoding signals more
than actually connecting.)
► **Red Flag:**
Disagreeing with her = chaos.
Any conflict becomes personal.
You're always the villain.

STRAIGHT FROM THE MAN MANUAL (THE **Emotional** EDITION)
If you're constantly tiptoeing around her moods,
you're not building a relationship —
you're dodging landmines in a minefield she planted.

RATE YOUR WOMAN
Emotional Stability

Name/Nickname	Score (1–10)	Quick Example or Story
Wife	8	Strong but steady. Cries, reflects, then circles back.
Girlfriend	6	Mostly stable... until conflict hits. Then it's silence for days.
Ex	2	Every issue became a courtroom trial — and I was always guilty.
Sister	9	Emotionally honest, even under pressure. Should teach classes.

No-O-Meter
Emotional Stability EDITION

✔ Can handle conflict without spiraling → +2
✔ Talks through emotions without blaming → +2
✔ Owns her triggers and apologizes

when needed → +2

✔ Can be vulnerable *and* respectful → +1

✔ Allows space for your emotions too → +1

✘ Weaponizes tears, guilt, or withdrawal → –2

✘ Shuts down or lashes out in conflict → –2

✘ Blames others for her moods → –1

✘ Uses "I'm emotional" as an excuse → –1

Add it up. Then ask:
Does she create calm — or chaos?

IF SHE SCORES A 9 OR 10...
That's not just a green flag —
that's a safe harbor in a messy world.
Respect her. Cherish her. Match her.

IF SHE SCORES A 3 OR BELOW...
If you're always bracing for the next emotional swing,
this isn't a relationship.
It's a rollercoaster with no lap bar.

YOUR NOTES, RANTS, OR PRAISE
*If her emotions always take center stage —
and yours are just backup dancers —
you're not partners. You're props.*

PART 2

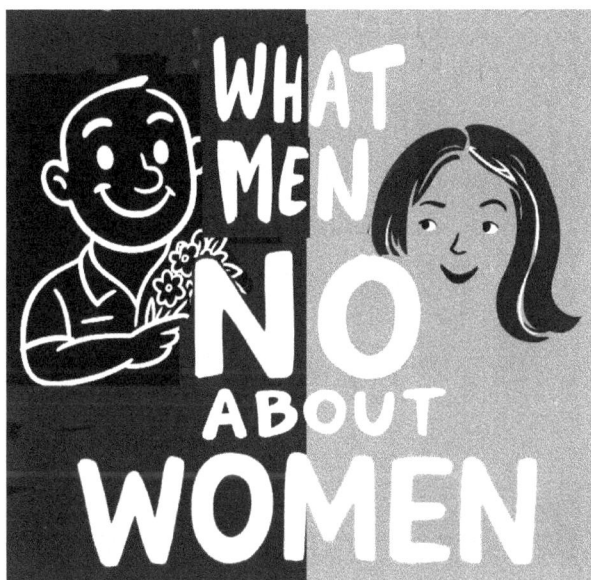

Tools, Truths & Takeaways

Now that you've laughed, ranted,
and rated... here's what to do
with it all.

Chapter **12**

Tools

"Because no one hands you a manual . . . here's the next best thing."

Tool # 1

THE
95/5
TECHNIQUE

How to Quit Fighting Over Nonsense and Actually Hear What She's Trying to Say,

Here's what I've learned after a lifetime of relationships (and several emotionally risky wallpaper projects):

95% of what you argue about is surface noise. The other 5%? That's where the real issue—and the connection—live.

Let's break it down *before* she storms out over the way you folded the towels.

The *95* %

The little things that get way too loud:
- That look she gave when you said, "Relax."
- The fact that you didn't notice her new haircut.

- That time you *thought* you were helping... but somehow made it worse.

This stuff is like static on the radio. It's annoying. But it's not the station she's trying to play.

The 5%

The real message underneath the noise:
- She wants to feel heard.
- She wants to feel important—not like an afterthought.
- She wants to know you *see* her, even when she's not talking.

Most of the time, it's not about the dishes or the volume of your chewing. It's about whether she feels valued in the relationship.

My Personal Example
(So You Don't Feel Alone)
(Because even I got it wrong sometimes)

Sonja and I once nearly went to war over a paint color. I said "eggshell." She said "ivory."

I thought they were the same. She thought I was hopeless.

What we were *really* fighting about? She didn't feel like I cared enough to be part of the decision. I didn't realize she needed support — not design input.

The 95%: Paint shade.

The 5%: Partnership and presence.

How to Use the 95/5 Technique
(Before You Dig Yourself Deeper)

1. **Pause.**
   Take a beat. Don't react. Don't roll your eyes. Just breathe.
2. **Ask Yourself:**
   "What's really going on here?"
   If your answer is "She's crazy," try again. That's still the 95%.
3. **Look for the Feeling.**
   What emotion is underneath the words? Disappointment? Feeling dismissed? Not feeling chosen?
4. **Respond to That.**
   Don't defend your tone. Don't argue about the laundry. Speak to the *heart* of it.

Quick Activity
(If You're Brave)

(If You're Brave Enough)

- Think of a recent argument that made you want to go sleep in the car.
- Write down what it seemed to be about (the 95%).
- Then write down what it was *really* about (the 5%).
- Ask: *How different would it have been if I had responded to the 5% instead?*

When to Pull This Out of Your Toolkit

"On a scale of 1 to 10, how big is this for you?"
(Then **listen** like the remote is broken
and your phone's dead.)

Dating?
Use it before you start racking up emotional
overdraft fees.

Living together?
Use it weekly. Sometimes hourly.

Married for decades?
This is how you avoid turning into glorified roommates
with joint tax returns.

Remember:
You can either be right about the 95%
or be connected around the 5%.
Pick wisely.

Tool #2

THE EMOTIONAL RICHTER SCALE

"Use numbers, not yelling."

"Use numbers, not guesswork."

Her emotions get loud. And complicated.

She says, "I'm upset."

You hear: "You're attacking me."

She says, "I'm fine."

You think: "Sweet, I'll go mow the lawn."

Let's fix that.

Instead of trying to read her tone like it's a puzzle on 'Jeopardy,' ask her to give you a number.

Yes—a number.

How it works:

She assigns a number (1–10) to how strongly she's feeling. Then says something like:

"This is an 8.5 for me emotionally. Can you see how important it is?"

Boom. Instant clarity. Fewer landmines.

Number	What It Means
1–2	Mild annoyance. Don't stress. Fixable.
3–4	She's frustrated. Pay attention.
5–6	Hurt feelings. You *need* to care.
7–8	High emotional impact. Stop multitasking and listen.
9–10	Crisis. Drop everything. This is deep.

Why it works:

- Stops the guessing game
- Shifts you out of defense mode
- Shows her you *want* to get it right (huge points)

TRY THIS PHRASE:

"On a scale of 1 to 10, how big is this for you?"

(Then **listen** like the remote is broken
and your phone's dead.)

The Emotional Richter Scale

Because Not All Drama is Actually Drama

Look, not every disagreement is a DEFCON 1 emergency. But some are.

And if you treat her "This really matters to me" moment like it's about the remote control?

Congratulations—you just escalated a 3.0 to an 8.7. This scale is your radar.

To know when to lean in—and when to stop talking. Let's break it down.

Magnitude 1.0 – 2.0
The "Not a Big Deal... Yet" Moment
- She's a little annoyed you didn't rinse your dish.
- It's not a fight.
- Just say, "Got it," and move on. You're fine.

Magnitude 2.1 – 3.0
The "You Weren't Listening" Vibe
- She mentioned dinner plans. Twice.
- You forgot. Again.
- You're not in trouble—just not helping your case.

Magnitude 3.1 – 4.0
The "This Happens a Lot" Frustration
- She's been repeating herself.
- You've been tuning out.

- She's wondering if she's speaking Wi-Fi and you're stuck on dial-up.

Magnitude 4.1 – 5.0
The "Why Am I Always the One?" Talk
- She feels like she's doing all the emotional heavy lifting.
- You thought things were fine.
- Time to step up and show her she's not alone.

Magnitude 5.1 – 6.0
The "This Actually Hurt" Reveal
- Maybe it was something you said. Or didn't say.
- She's not yelling. She's withdrawing.
- Time to sit down, shut up, and really listen.

Magnitude 6.1 – 7.0
The Silent Treatment Earthquake
- It started with a sigh.
- Now she's going quiet.
- That's not peace—it's pressure building.

Magnitude 7.1 – 8.0
The "Do You Even See Me?" Breakdown
- She's questioning if you're present.
- Emotionally. Mentally. Physically.
- She needs connection—not just another promise to do better.

Magnitude 8.1 – 9.0
The "I'm Not Okay" Confession
- She opens up. She's raw. She's crying.
- This isn't a fix-it moment. It's a *hold-her* moment.

- Don't analyze. Empathize.

Magnitude 9.1 – 10.0
The "We Might Not Make It" Storm

- She's overwhelmed. Burned out. Maybe feeling unseen for a long time.
- This is where you show up fully—or risk losing her.

David's Note:

"Guys—most of these emotional 'quakes' aren't about the cabinets or the calendar.

They're about being heard. Respected. Understood. If she says it's a 9, don't ask why she's overreacting. Ask what you missed the first time."

Quick Tip:

When she's heated, try this:

**"I can tell this matters.
What number would you give it?"**

She'll be surprised you asked. And grateful you cared.

Final Thought:

You don't have to be perfect. Just present. And if you show her that her emotions *matter*, you'll calm more storms than you'll ever cause.

Chapter **13**

FINAL Score Card & Reflection

**Time to tally the truth—
and maybe text your brother, your
barber, or that one friend who always
says "Dude, she's not the one."**

(Or your bestie. Or your group chat titled
'Avoid This One'.)

YOUR TOP 3 WOMEN

Grab your highest-scoring ladies from the
NO-o-Meter charts.

Then decide where they land:
Keeper, Maybe, or Nope.

Name/Nickname	Total Score (Out of 110)	Verdict
		☐ Keeper ☐ Maybe ☐ Nope
		☐ Keeper ☐ Maybe ☐ Nope
		☐ Keeper ☐ Maybe ☐ Nope

WHAT I LEARNED
I want more of:

I'm done tolerating:

I thought I wanted

...but I actually need

My emotional Richter scale will now include:

BONUS 1

RANTS, NOTES & FINAL THOUGHTS

Say What You REALLY Wanted to Say (But Didn't)

This is the page for that thing you *almost* said...
...then remembered you like having peace in your house.

---Maybe it was during a fight.
---Maybe it was when she said "I'm fine" in that tone that meant **she's absolutely not fine**.
---Maybe it was when she asked, "Do you even know what I'm feeling right now?" and you *definitely* didn't.
---This is the stuff you couldn't text.
---Wouldn't post.
---And sure as hell didn't bring up over dinner with her parents.

So go ahead—rant it out.
Be honest. Be messy. Be you.
This page doesn't judge (and it doesn't screenshot).

Whether it turns into your next therapy script or just clears space in your head...

Say it here.
Before it says itself at the worst possible time.

_____

_____

_____

_____

_____

_____

_____

_____

_____

_____

BONUS 2

No-O-Meter

NO-O-METER WALL OF FAME (OR SHAME)
Welcome to the Hall of "She Did WHAT?"

Some women leave a glow.

Others leave you double-checking your phone plan and rethinking your life choices.

This is your moment to reflect, laugh, or gently roast the women who taught you what *really* matters—and what to walk away from.

Use this page for insight, healing... or entertainment.

Score each one on the legendary NO-o-Meter:
1 = Sweet memory | 10 = Emotional arson

Category	Name/Nickname	What She Did	NO-o-Meter Score (1–10)
Most Emotionally Available			
Funniest Woman			
Best First Impression / Worst Follow-Through			
Most Confusing Communicator			
She Meant Well, Probably			
"No Further Contact Needed" Award			

BONUS 3
STICKY NOTE TRUTHS
Sticky Notes from My Brain

Sometimes, clarity hits like a lightning bolt. Other times, it arrives at 2am while staring at the ceiling or watching reruns of *Top Gear*.

This is your space to jot down those "Wait... was that a red flag?" moments, truths you wish you knew sooner, or things you should've said—but didn't.

Bonus points for sarcasm, honesty, or poetic pettiness. Examples:

• "She said she didn't want anything for her birthday. She   lied."
• "Never argue with someone who screenshots for sport."
• "Her 'I'm fine' came with a plot twist."
Now your turn:

BONUS 4
REVIEW, REFLECT & SHARE IT FOR THE NEXT GUY

Did This Book Make You Laugh, Think, or Rethink
Every Woman You've Ever Dated?

Then please leave a review!

Your words might be the wake-up call
another guy needs.

Reviews help this book reach more honest, curious,
emotionally evolving men just like you.

Amazon / Goodreads / Wherever Men Go to Reflect
(preferably not in a group chat)

*"This book made me laugh, cringe, and reconsider that
one 'cool girl' who ghosted me after brunch."*

*"It's like relationship therapy...
without the eye contact."*

*"10/10 would recommend. Also, I texted my ex 'Thank
you. I finally get it.' She didn't respond. Still worth it."*

Thank you!

Final Word from David

"Every guy I know has a list—hot, cool, likes football, doesn't hate his friends. But the wise ones? They learned to revise it.

You deserve respect, laughter, peace—and a woman who doesn't make you feel like you're always one wrong word away from a TED Talk on emotional maturity.

And if you haven't found her yet? Maybe you're busy becoming the kind of man who knows what to do when he does.

Here's the deal: most couples spend years fighting over dumb stuff and wondering why they're still stuck. Don't be most couples.

You won't always say the right thing. You won't always understand what's going on (spoiler: sometimes she doesn't either). But you can choose whether to react like a grown-up... or like the world's most dramatic contestant on *The Bachelor*.

These tools won't make you perfect. But they might save you from another "We need to talk" dinner, a weekend of silent treatment, or an emergency trip to buy apology flowers because you thought she was "just being emotional."

Use them well. Listen with your whole self. Say sorry like you mean it.And for the love of good relationships— keep showing up, even when it's hard.

With respect, a grin, and the belief that you're capable of more than just 'getting by,'

—David"

The Businessman and Entrepreneur in the USA

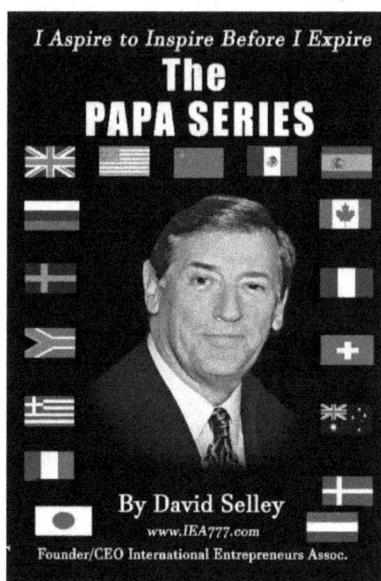

I Aspire to Inspire Before I Expire
The PAPA SERIES
By David Selley
www.IEA777.com
Founder/CEO International Entrepreneurs Assoc.

**David Selley's PAPA Book Series:
A Guinness World Record Journey**

David Selley's PAPA Book Series is more than a collection of stories—it's a testament to a life fully lived, spanning three continents and more than eight decades of family, business, and personal growth. Part of his

Guinness World Record attempt to become the oldest author to publish the most books in a single year, the series captures the wisdom, resilience, and entrepreneurial spirit that have defined his extraordinary journey.

From a tough childhood in England, to transformative years in Canada, to entrepreneurial success in the USA, David's books blend memoir, business insights, and timeless life lessons. At the heart of it all is his 65-year marriage—a remarkable story of love, perseverance, and true partnership.

Beyond the personal stories, David's latest venture, the **International Entrepreneur Association (IEA)**, offers a fresh vision for global business networking. By connecting importers and exporters through a streamlined system, he aims to open new opportunities for businesses around the world.

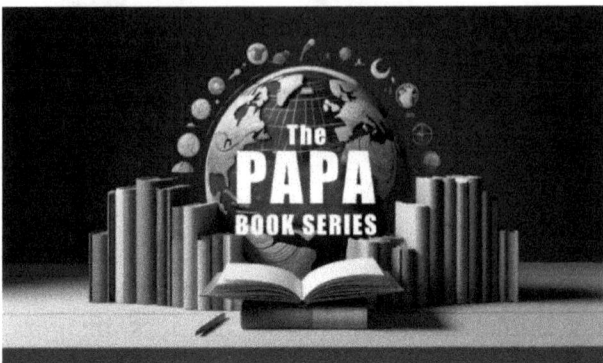

COMPLETE SERIES TITLES

(Includes books newly released or publishing soon)

PAPA #1 – The Boy in England: Growing Up Tough
A tale of resilience and survival from David's early days in post-war England.

PAPA #2 – The Young Man in Canada
A vivid look at his transformative years in Canada, filled with personal and professional growth.

PAPA #3 – The Businessman and Entrepreneur in the USA - Chronicles David's entry into the business world and his entrepreneurial adventures in the U.S..

PAPA #4 – The Entrepreneur: Papa's Secret #4
A deep dive into his entrepreneurial mindset and the lessons learned from building businesses.

PAPA #5 – Three Lives, Three Lands
A condensed journey through David Selley's life in England, Canada, and the USA.

SERIES TITLES - *continued*

PAPA #6 – Married Forever: The Four Seasons of Marriage - Reflects on the evolving phases of marriage over 65+ years, from spring to winter.

PAPA #7 – The Father
Explores David's journey as a father, filled with challenges, love, and important lessons.

PAPA #8 – The Grandfather: Leaving a Legacy
A heartwarming tribute to family and the importance of passing down wisdom and values.

PAPA #9 – Health, Wealth & Happiness: You Can Have All Three - A practical guide to achieving balance and abundance in life—covering the essentials of personal health, financial well-being, and lasting happiness.

PAPA #10 – The Investor: Nothing Down Real Estate... Yes! It Works - Presents proven strategies for real estate investing without upfront costs.

PAPA #11 – The Famous 50 Book Series
An exciting global vanity publishing project, connecting notable people across industries at www.famous50.com.

PAPA #12 – GenMar: The Generational Marketing Advantage - Reveals how understanding generational values can transform marketing and deepen customer connection.

SERIES TITLES - *continued*

PAPA #13 – What Women NO About Men

A witty, honest look at the ten traits women want in a man (plus one that changes everything), helping readers spot red flags and laugh along the way.

PAPA #14 – Boundaries with Benefits

A practical, cheeky journal for women to get clear on their "NOs," build better boundaries, and protect their peace with humor and heart.

PAPA #15 – What Men NO About Women

A humorous, eye-opening guide revealing what women want—and what they mean when they say, "I'm fine." With 10 traits (plus one that changes everything), it's part decoder, part reality check, and fully practical.

PAPA #16 – Left vs. Right: American Politics

A bold look at the political divide—why it exists, how it shapes daily life, and what we can do about it. Whether you lean left, right, or somewhere in between, it invites civil reflection in uncivil times.

PAPA #17 – Immigration: Legal Turmoil?

A fact-based look at one of America's most divisive issues. As an immigrant turned proud U.S. citizen, David shares the history, laws, and human stories that reveal immigration's real impact on the nation's future.

PAPA #18 – One Year, 18 Books: My Guinness World Record Attempt -

A behind-the-scenes look at David Selley's ambitious year-long challenge to set a

Guinness World Record.

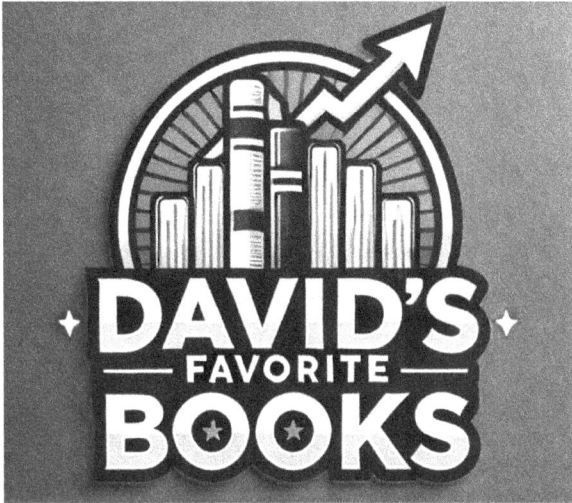

"How to Win Friends and Influence People"
by Dale Carnegie

"The Magic of Thinking Big"
by David J. Schwartz

"Think and Grow Rich"
by Napoleon Hill

"The Power of Positive Thinking"
by Norman Vincent Peale

"The Power of Focus"
by Jack Canfield, Mark Victor Hansen, and Les Hewitt

David's Favorite Books - *Continued*

"The Aladdin Factor"
by Jack Canfield and Mark Victor Hansen

"Innovation and Entrepreneurship"
by Peter F. Drucker

"Secrets of Power Negotiating"
by Roger Dawson

"See You at the Top"
by Zig Ziglar

"Live Your Dreams"
by Les Brown

The Art of Exceptional Living"
by Jim Rohn

**"Maximum Achievement:
Strategies and Skills That Will Unlock
Your Hidden Powers"**
by Brian Tracy

"The 21 Irrefutable Laws of Leadership"
by John C. Maxwell

My Creed

By Dean Alfange

A powerful declaration of
self-reliance, entrepreneurship and personal freedom.

I do not choose to be a common man,
It is my right to be uncommon ... if I can,
I seek opportunity ... not security.
I do not wish to be a kept citizen.
Humbled and dulled by having the
State look after me.
I want to take the calculated risk;
To dream and to build.
To fail and to succeed.
I refuse to barter incentive for a dole;
I prefer the challenges of life
To the guaranteed existence;
The thrill of fulfillment
To the stale calm of Utopia.
I will not trade freedom for beneficence
Nor my dignity for a handout
I will never cower before any master
Nor bend to any threat.
It is my heritage to stand erect.
Proud and unafraid;
To think and act for myself,
To enjoy the benefit of my creations
And to face the world boldly and say:
This, with God's help, I have done.

All this is what it means to be an
"Entrepreneur."

About the Author

David Selley

David Selley is an 87-year-old author, entrepreneur, and unapologetic truth-teller with a talent for saying what most men are still trying to decode. With a lifetime of personal stories, relationship lessons, and cheeky humor, David writes books that are part wake-up call, part survival guide—and always rooted in truth.

He's the author of *Married Forever: The Four Seasons of Marriage*, a heartfelt look at long-term love inspired by his own 65+ year marriage. His writing is known for its clarity, humor, and the kind of honest insight that makes you laugh, nod, and sometimes cringe.

This book, *What Men NO About Women*, is a companion

to *What Women NO About Men*—two witty, no-fluff guides designed to help both sexes understand each other just a little bit better. Together, they're part of David's bold mission: to break a Guinness World Record by becoming the oldest man to publish the most books in a single   year.
(Yes, he's still competitive. And still married.)

David continues to write, mentor, and marvel at how confusing—and beautiful—relationships can be when men actually start paying attention.

Find more of his books, tools, and truth bombs at:

Contact David Selley
www.iea777.com
davidselley08@gmail.com
1-800-388-3102

Disclaimer: This book is part of David Selley's personal attempt to set a Guinness World Record for publishing the most books in one year. It is an independent effort and is not sponsored, endorsed, or officially affiliated with Guinness World Records™.